Disney's
My First Songbook

A Treasury of Favorite Songs to Sing and Play

DISNEY PRESS

New York

HAL•LEONARD® CORPORATION

7777 W. BLUEMOUND RD. P.O. BOX 13819 MILWAUKEE, WI 53213

Contents

Cruella De Vil

From Walt Disney's *101 Dalmatians*

Words and Music by Mel Leven

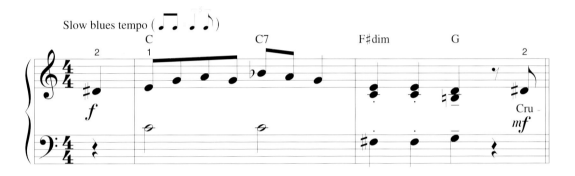

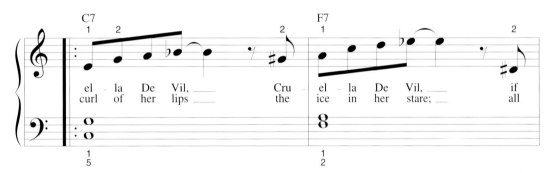

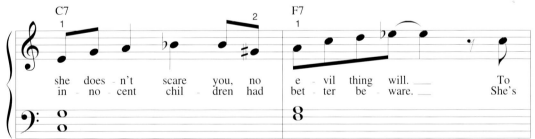

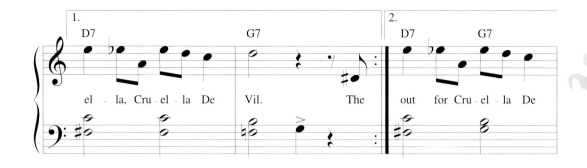

1.
D7 · · · G7 · · ·
el - la, Cru - el - la De · · · Vil. · · · The

2.
D7 · · · G7 · · ·
out · · · for Cru - el - la De

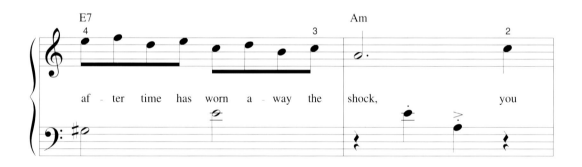

C · · · E7 · · · Am
Vil. · · · At · first you think Cru - el - la · is the · dev - il, · but

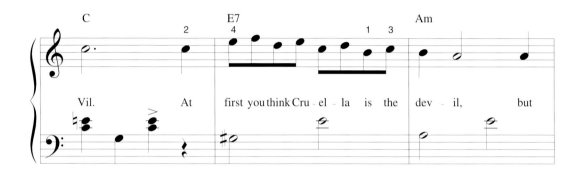

E7 · · · Am
af - ter time has worn a - way the · shock, · · · you

D7
come · to · re - al - ize · · · you've · seen her kind of eyes

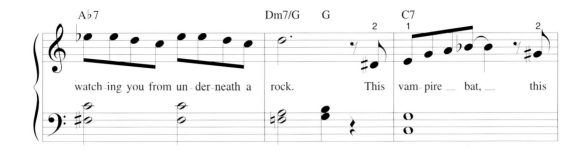

watch-ing you from un-der-neath a rock. This vam-pire __ bat, __ this

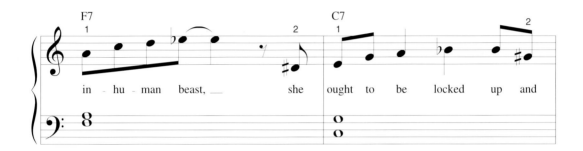

in - hu - man beast, __ she ought to be locked up and

nev - er re - leased. __ The world was such a whole-some place un -

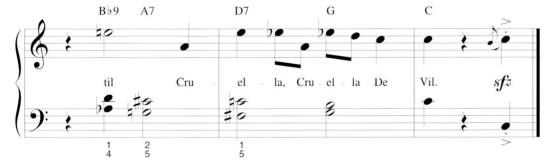

til Cru - el - la, Cru-el - la De Vil.

A Whole New World

From Walt Disney's *Aladdin*

Music by Alan Menken • Lyrics by Tim Rice

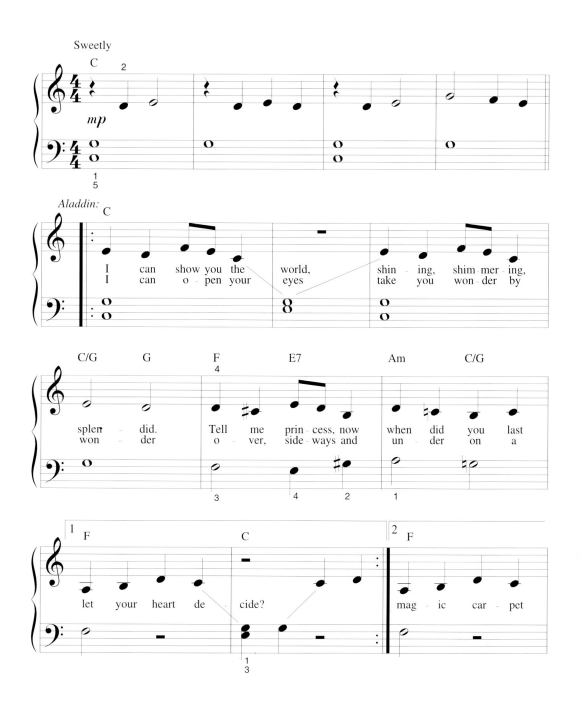

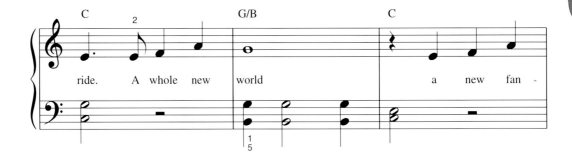

ride.   A whole new world

a new fan -

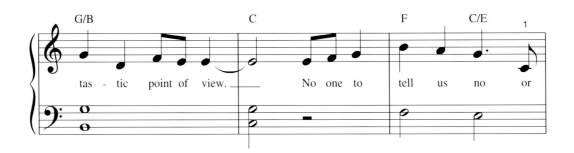

tas - tic   point of view.____   No one to   tell   us   no   or

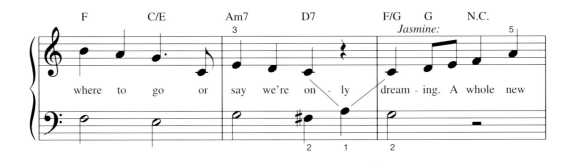

where   to   go   or   say   we're   on - ly   dream - ing.   A whole new

world   a   daz - zling   place   I   nev - er   knew.____

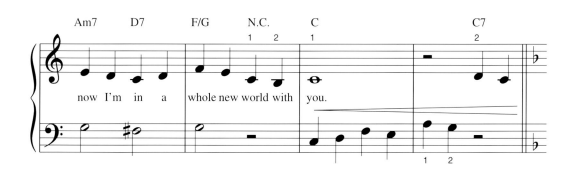

But when I'm 'way up here it's crys - tal clear that

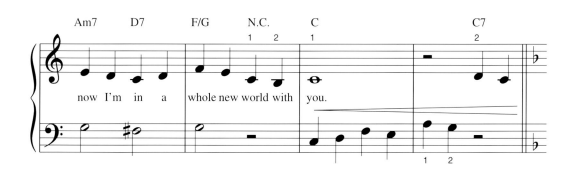

now I'm in a whole new world with you.

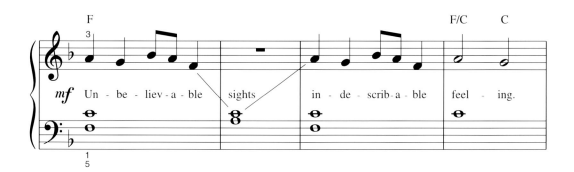

mf Un - be - liev - a - ble sights in - de - scrib - a - ble feel - ing.

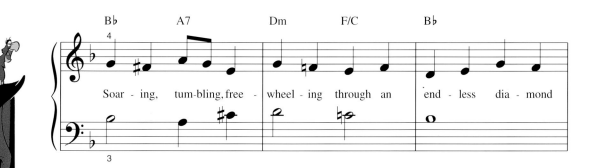

Soar - ing, tum - bling, free - wheel - ing through an end - less dia - mond

sky. A whole new world, _____ a hun - dred thou - sand things to see.

___ I'm like a shoot - ing star. I've come so far I

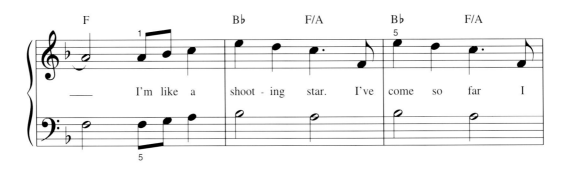

can't go back to where I used to be. Ev - 'ry turn a sur -

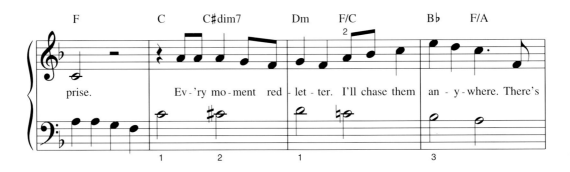

prise. Ev - 'ry mo - ment red - let - ter. I'll chase them an - y - where. There's

time to spare. Let me share this whole new world with

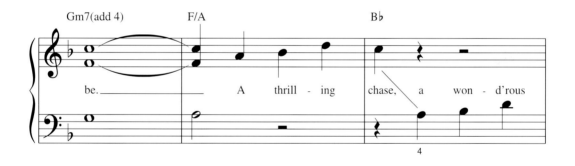

you. A whole new world, that's where we'll

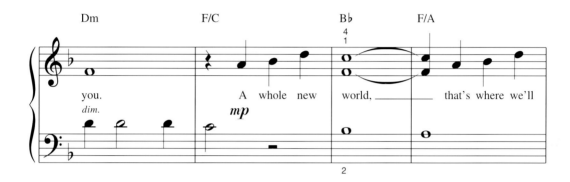

be. A thrill - ing chase, a won - d'rous

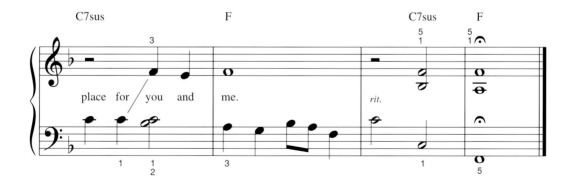

place for you and me.

The Bare Necessities

From Walt Disney's *The Jungle Book*

Words and Music by Terry Gilkyson

Look for the bare ne - ces - si - ties, the simple bare ne - ces - si - ties, for - get a - bout your wor - ries and your strife. I mean the

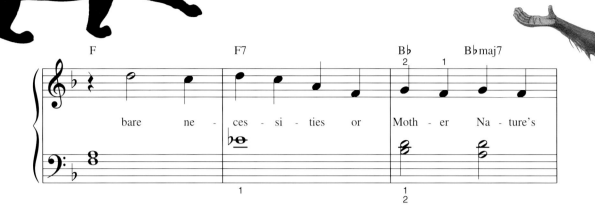

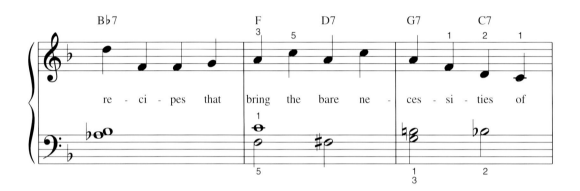

bare ne - ces - si - ties or Moth - er Na - ture's

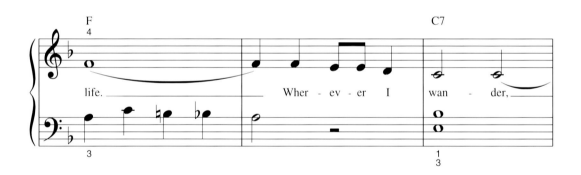

re - ci - pes that bring the bare ne - ces - si - ties of

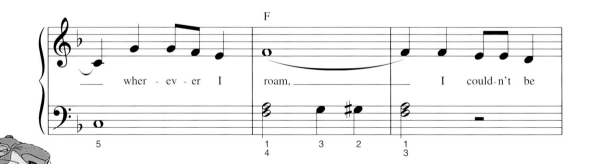

life. ___ Wher - ev - er I wan - der, ___

___ wher - ev - er I roam, ___ I could - n't be

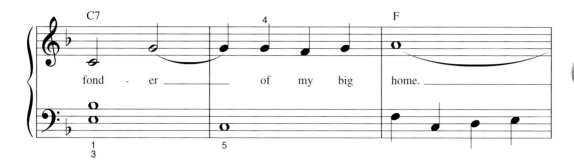

fond - er _____ of my big home. _____

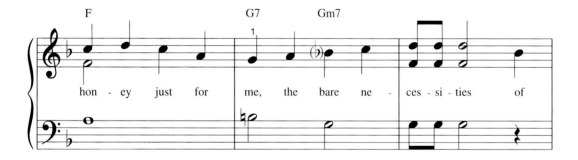

_____ The bees are buzz - in' in the tree to make some

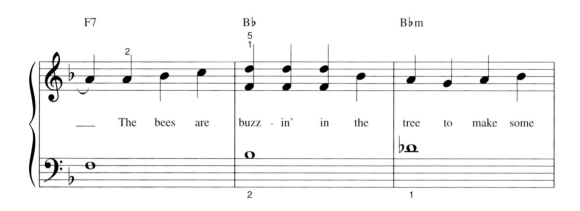

hon - ey just for me, the bare ne - ces - si - ties of

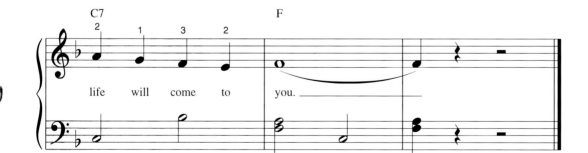

life will come to you. _____

Colors of the Wind

From Walt Disney's *Pocahontas*

Music by Alan Menken • Lyrics by Stephen Schwartz

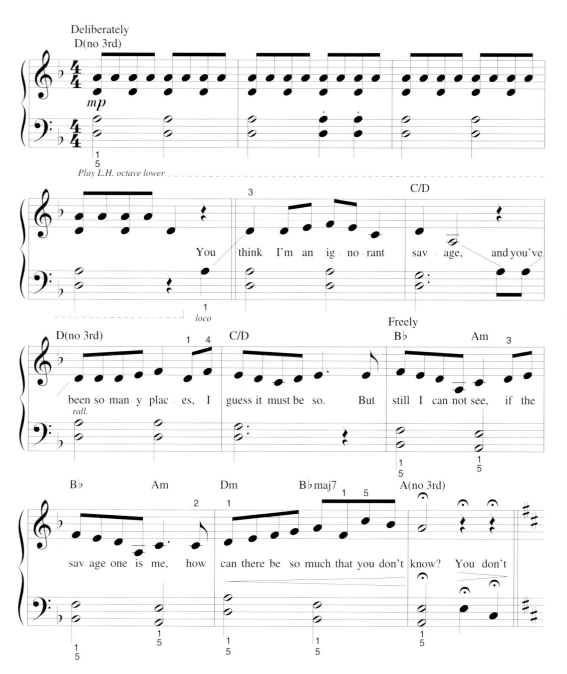

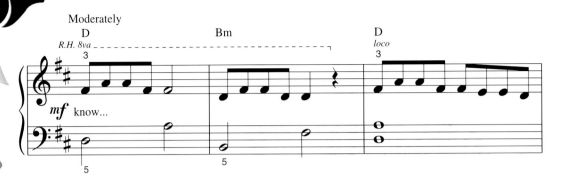

Moderately

D ... Bm ... D *loco*

mf know...

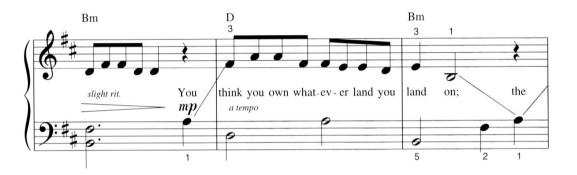

Bm ... D ... Bm

slight rit. ... *mp* ... *a tempo*

You think you own what-ev-er land you land on; the

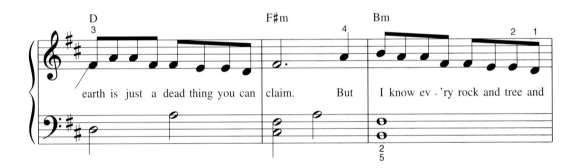

D ... F#m ... Bm

earth is just a dead thing you can claim. But I know ev-'ry rock and tree and

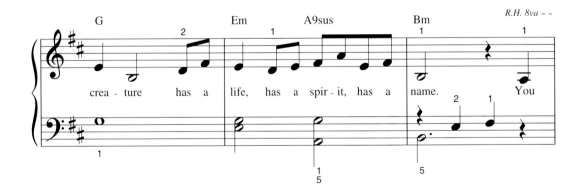

G ... Em ... A9sus ... Bm ... *R.H. 8va – –*

crea - ture has a life, has a spir - it, has a name. You

20

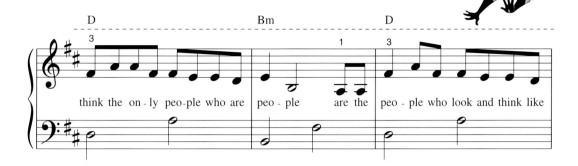

think the on - ly peo-ple who are | peo - ple | are the | peo - ple who look and think like

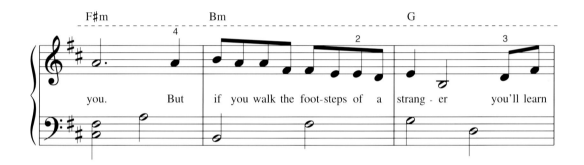

you. But | if you walk the foot-steps of a | strang - er | you'll learn

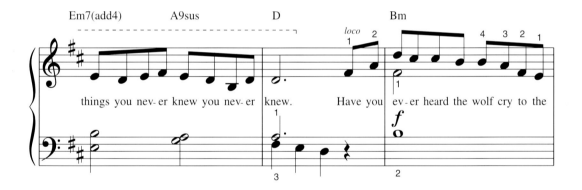

things you nev-er knew you nev-er | knew. Have you | ev-er heard the wolf cry to the

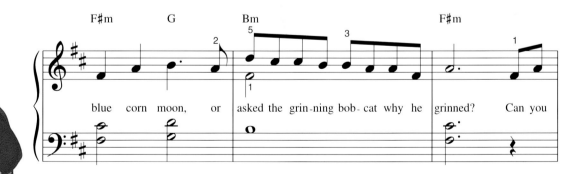

blue corn moon, or | asked the grin-ning bob- cat why he | grinned? Can you

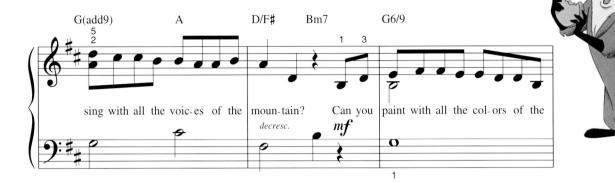

sing with all the voic-es of the moun-tain? Can you paint with all the col-ors of the

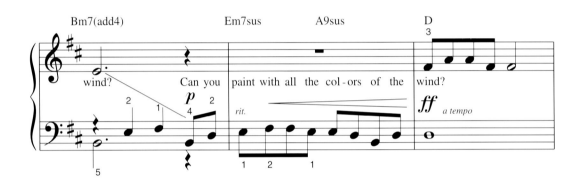

wind? Can you paint with all the col-ors of the wind?

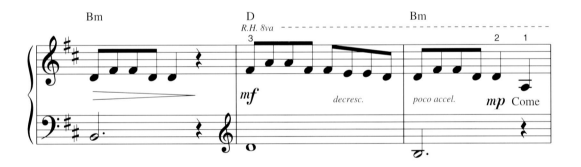

Come

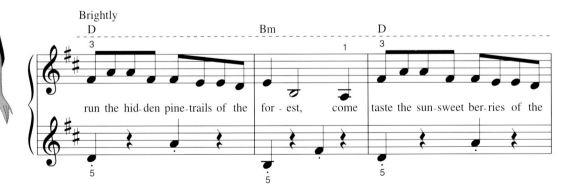

run the hid-den pine-trails of the for - est, come taste the sun-sweet ber-ries of the

F#m   Bm   Bm/A   G

earth.   Come   roll in all the rich-es all a-round you,   and for

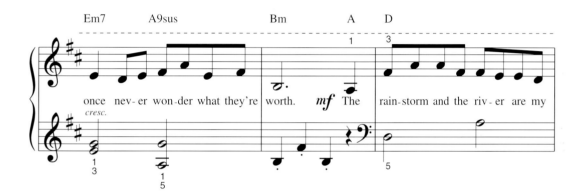

Em7   A9sus   Bm   A   D

once nev-er won-der what they're worth. *mf* The rain-storm and the riv-er are my

cresc.

Bm   D   F#m

bro-thers;   the   her-on and the ot-ter are my   friends;   and

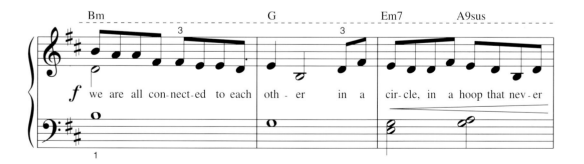

Bm   G   Em7   A9sus

f we are all con-nect-ed to each oth-er   in a   cir-cle, in a hoop that nev-er

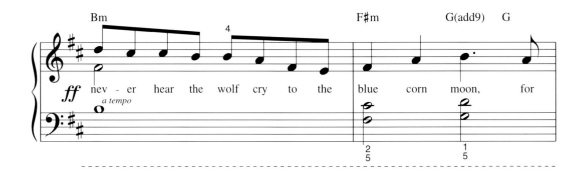

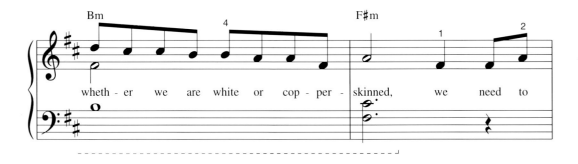

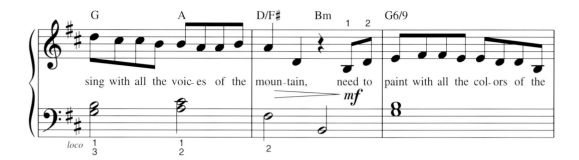

sing with all the voic-es of the moun-tain, need to paint with all the col-ors of the

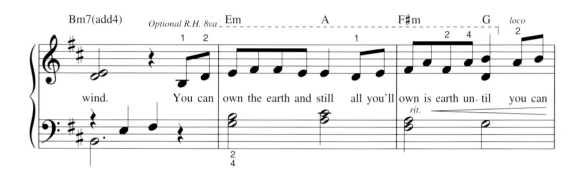

wind. You can own the earth and still all you'll own is earth un-til you can

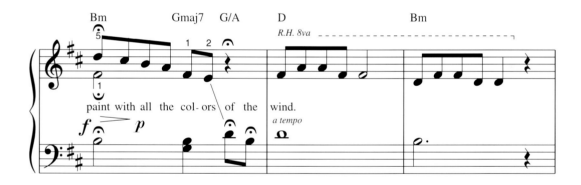

paint with all the col-ors of the wind.

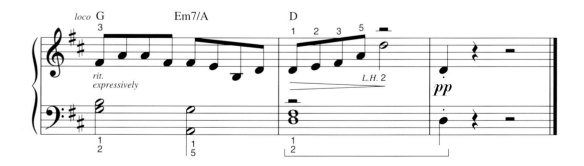

Under the Sea

From Walt Disney's *The Little Mermaid*

Lyrics by Howard Ashman • Music by Alan Menken

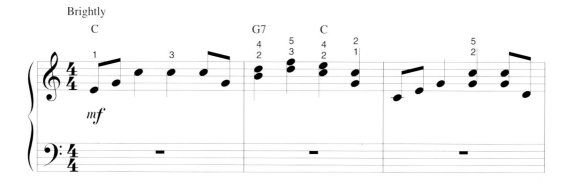

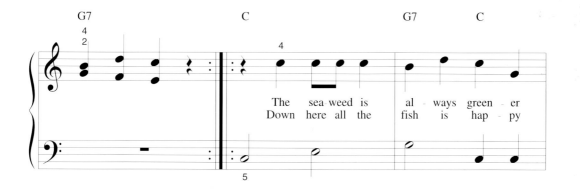

The sea-weed is al - ways green - er
Down here all the fish is hap - py

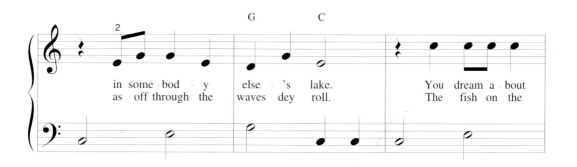

in some-bod - y else - 's lake.
as off through the waves dey roll.

You dream a - bout
The fish on the

go - ing   up   there.
land   ain't   hap - py.

But   that   is   a   big   mis - take.
They   sad 'cause they   in   the   bowl.

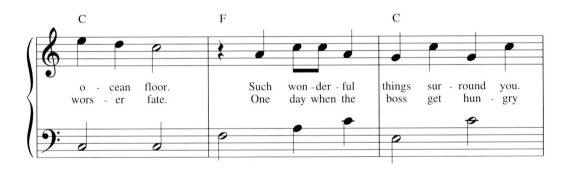

Just   look   at the   world   a - round   you,
But   fish   in the   bowl   is   luck - y,

right   here   on the
they   in   for a

o - cean   floor.
wors - er   fate.

Such   won - der - ful
One   day when the

things   sur - round   you.
boss   get   hun - gry

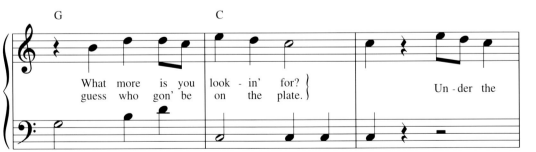

What   more   is you
guess   who   gon' be

look - in'   for?
on   the   plate.

Un - der the

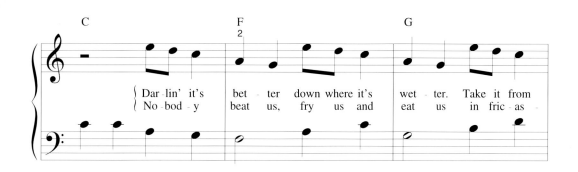

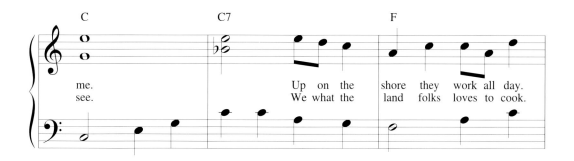

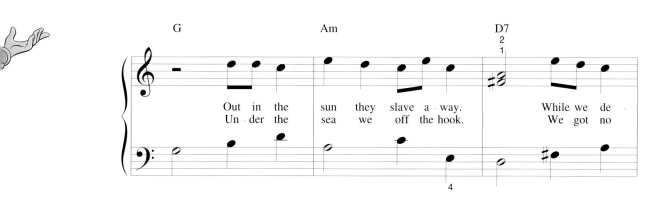

sea,   un - der the   sea.

Dar - lin' it's   bet - ter   down where it's   wet - ter.   Take it from
No - bod - y   beat us,   fry us and   eat   us   in fric - as -

me.   Up on the   shore   they   work all day.
see.   We what the   land   folks   loves to cook.

Out in the   sun   they   slave a - way.   While we   de -
Un - der the   sea   we   off the hook.   We got   no

vo - tin' full time to float - in' un -der the sea.
trou - bles life is the bub - bles un -der the

sea. Un - der the sea.

Since life is sweet here we got the beat here nat - u - ral -

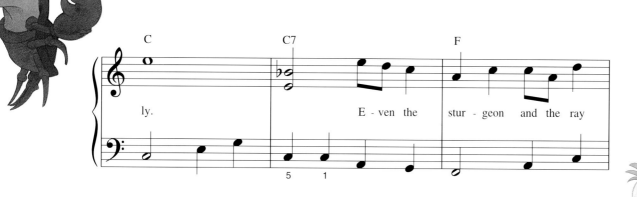

ly.

E - ven the stur - geon and the ray

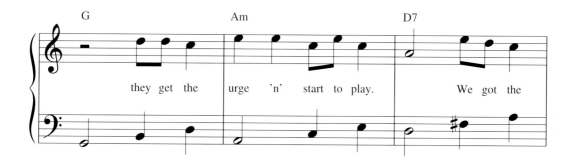

they get the urge 'n' start to play.

We got the

spir - it, you got to hear it un - der the sea.

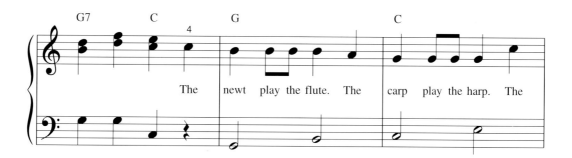

The newt play the flute. The carp play the harp. The

plaice play the bass. And they sound-in' sharp. The bass play the brass. The

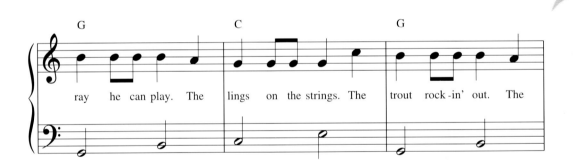

chub play the tub. The fluke is the duke of soul. The

G C G

ray he can play. The lings on the strings. The trout rock-in' out. The

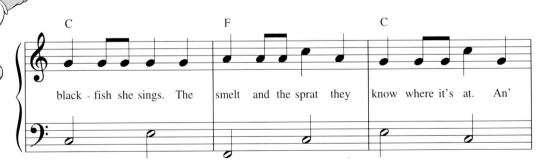

black - fish she sings. The smelt and the sprat they know where it's at. An'

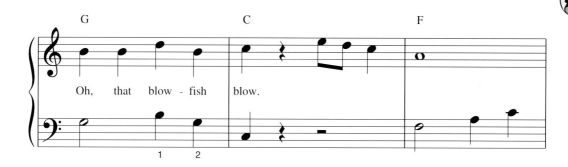

Oh,   that   blow - fish   blow.

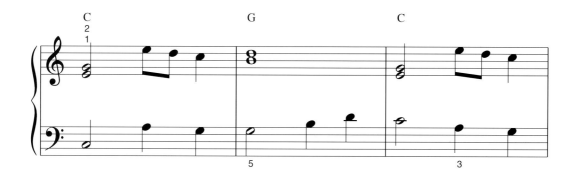

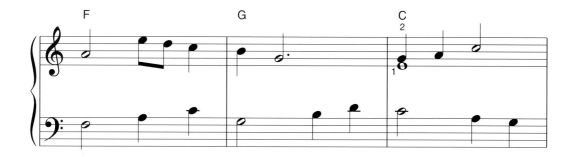

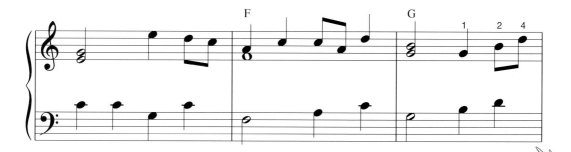

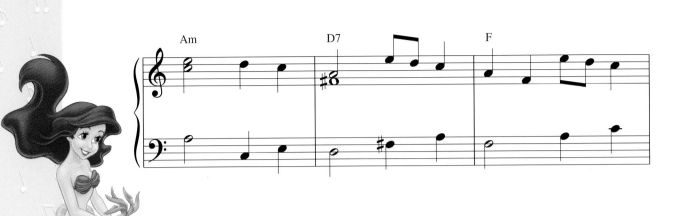

Un - der the

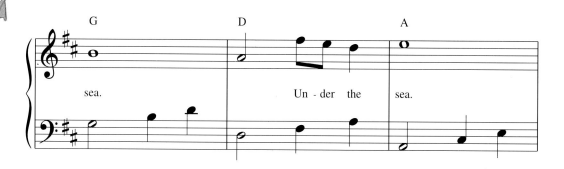

sea. Un - der the sea.

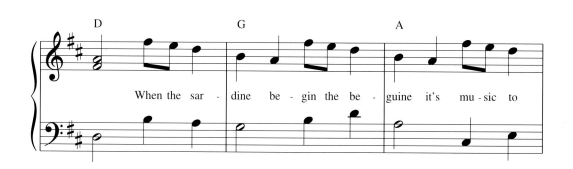

When the sar - dine be - gin the be - guine it's mu - sic to

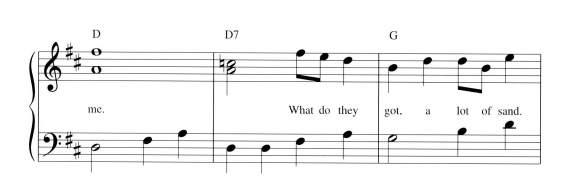

me. What do they got, a lot of sand.

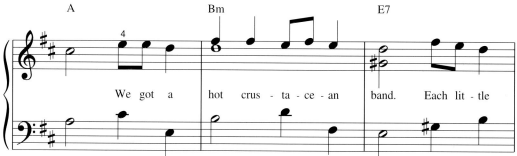

We got a hot crus - ta - ce - an band. Each lit - tle

35

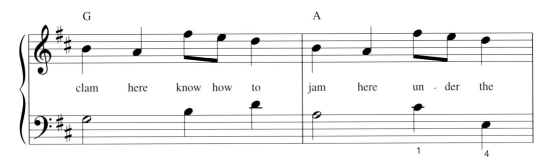

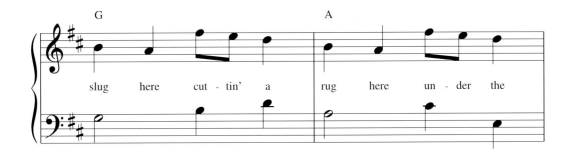

snail here know how to wail here. That's why it's

hot - ter un - der the wa - ter. Ya we in

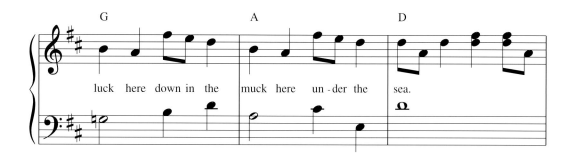

luck here down in the muck here un - der the sea.

Following the Leader

From Walt Disney's *Peter Pan*

Words by Ted Sears and Winston Hibler • Music by Oliver Wallace

Moderately (in 2)

Fol - low - ing the lead - er, the lead - er, the lead - er, we're

fol - low - ing the lead - er wher - ev - er he may go. _____ We

won't be home till morn - ing, till morn - ing, till morn - ing, we

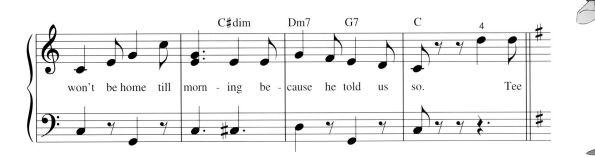

won't be home till morn - ing be - cause he told us so. Tee

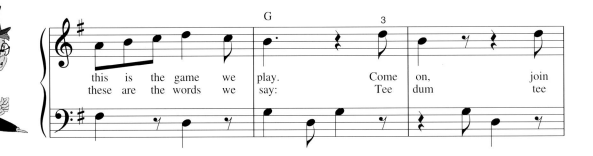

dum, tee dee, a tee - dle ee do tee
dum, tee dee, a tee - dle ee do tee

day. We're out for fun, and
day. We march a - long, and

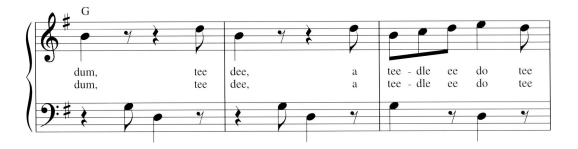

this is the game we play. Come on, join
these are the words we say: Tee dum tee

in and sing your trou-bles a - way with a
dee a tee - dle dee-dle dee - ay, oh, a

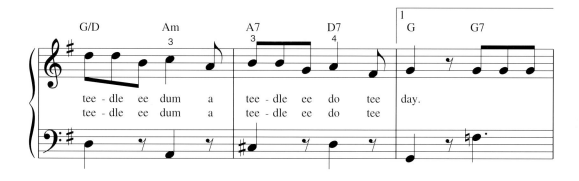

G/D   Am   A7   D7   G   G7

tee - dle ee dum a tee - dle ee do tee day.
tee - dle ee dum a tee - dle ee do tee

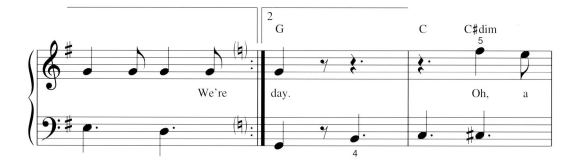

G   C   C#dim

We're day. Oh, a

G/D   Am   A7   D7   G

tee-dle ee dum a tee-dle ee do tee day.

You've Got a Friend in Me

From Walt Disney's *Toy Story*

Music and Lyrics by Randy Newman

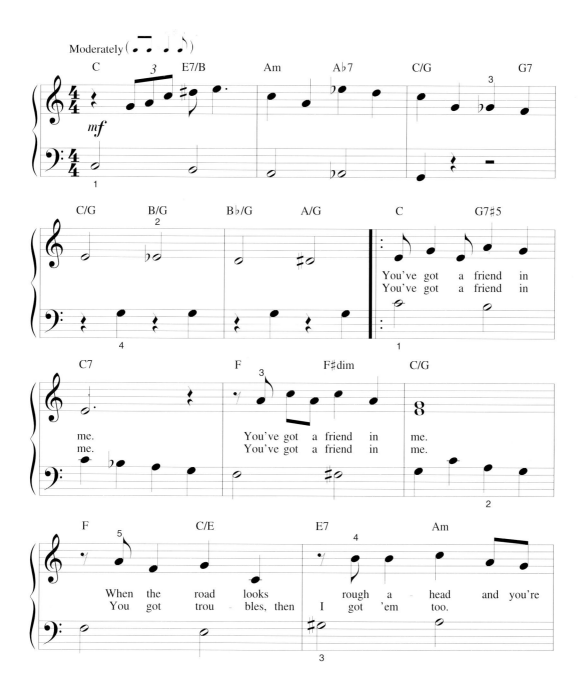

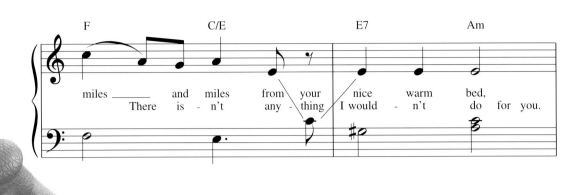

miles _____ and miles from your nice warm bed,
There is - n't any - thing I would - n't do for you.

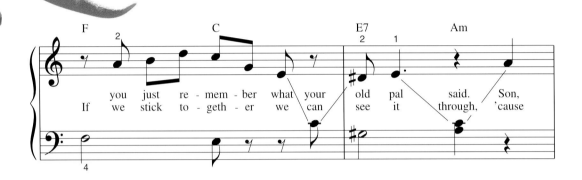

you just re - mem - ber what your old pal said. Son,
If we stick to - geth - er we can see it through, 'cause

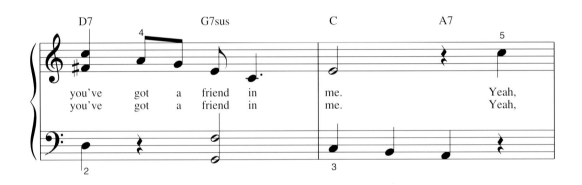

you've got a friend in me.
you've got a friend in me. Yeah,
Yeah,

1.

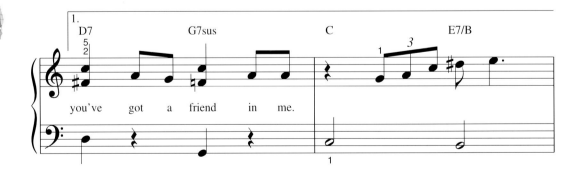

you've got a friend in me.

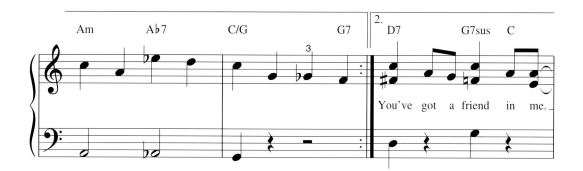

Am   A♭7   C/G   G7 |2. D7   G7sus   C

You've got a friend in me.

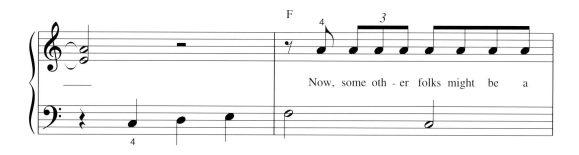

F

Now, some oth-er folks might be a

B   C6   B7

lit-tle bit smart-er than I am,   big-ger and strong-er

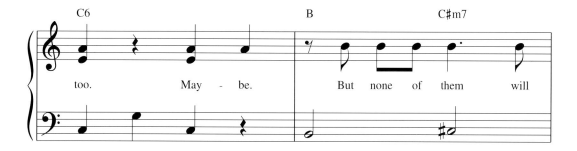

C6   B   C#m7

too.   May-be.   But none of them will

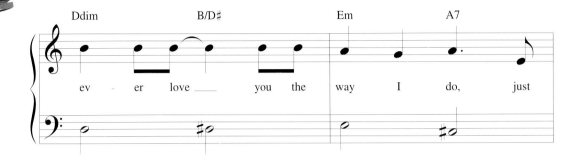

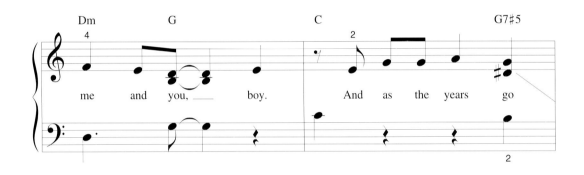

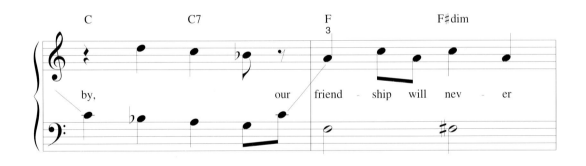

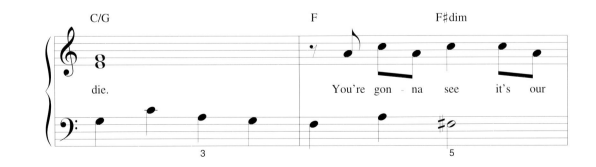

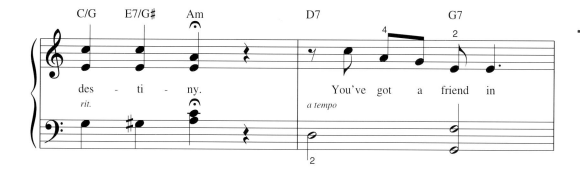

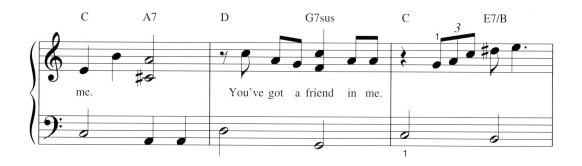

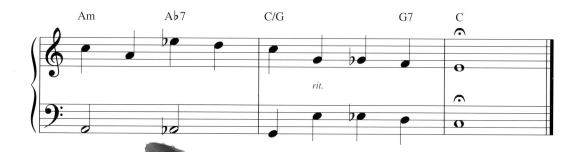

Once Upon a Dream

From Walt Disney's *Sleeping Beauty*

Words and Music by Sammy Fain and Jack Lawrence
Adapted from a Theme by Tchaikovsky

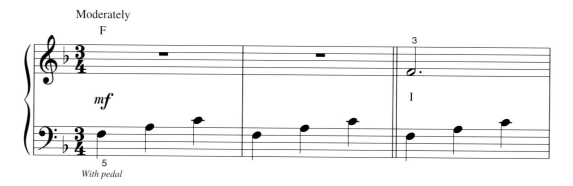

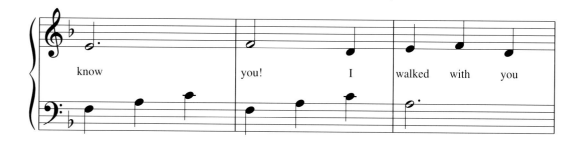

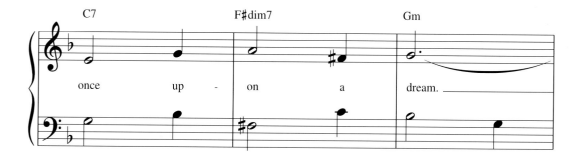

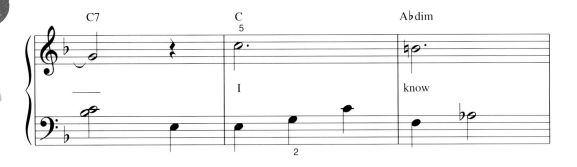

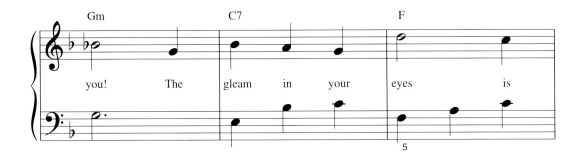

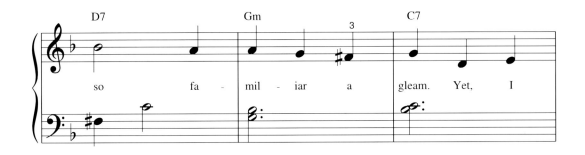

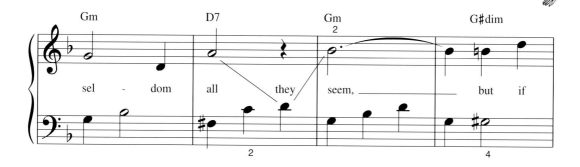

sel - dom all they seem, _____ but if

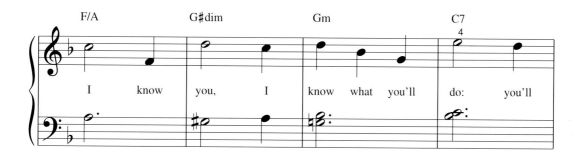

I know you, I know what you'll do: you'll

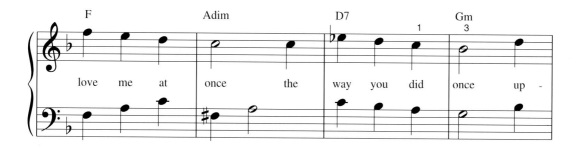

love me at once the way you did once up -

on a dream.
rit.

A Dream Is a Wish Your Heart Makes

From Walt Disney's *Cinderella*

Words and Music by Mack David, Al Hoffman and Jerry Livingston

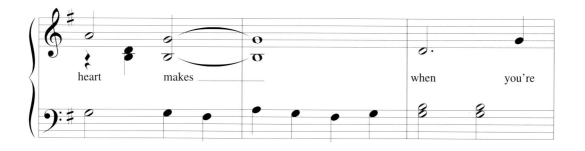

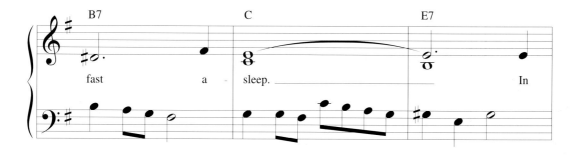

dreams   you   will   lose   your   heart - aches;

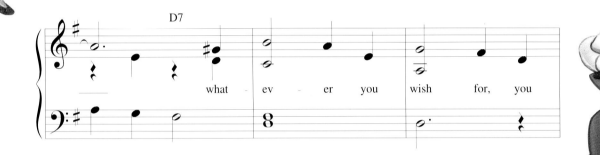

what - ev - er   you   wish   for,   you

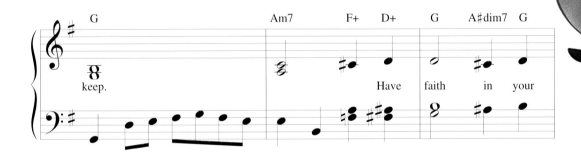

keep.   Have   faith   in   your

dreams   and   some   day   your

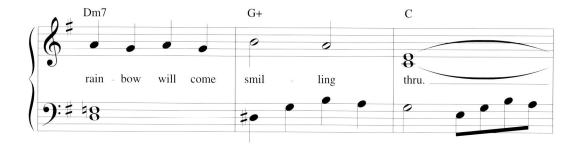

rain - bow will come smil - ling thru.

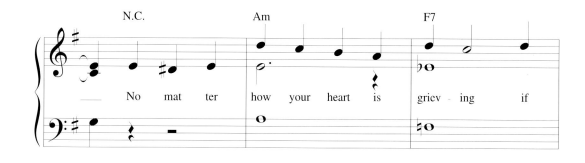

No mat - ter how your heart is griev - ing if

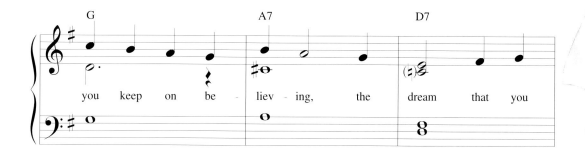

you keep on be - liev - ing, the dream that you

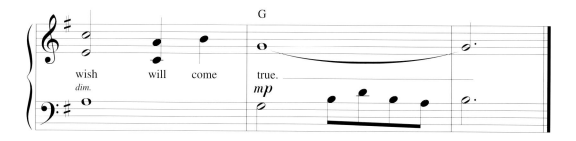

wish will come true.
dim. *mp*

Bibbidi-Bobbidi-Boo

(The Magic Song)

From Walt Disney's *Cinderella*

Words by Jerry Livingston • Music by Mack David and Al Hoffman

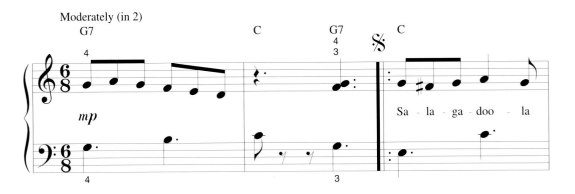

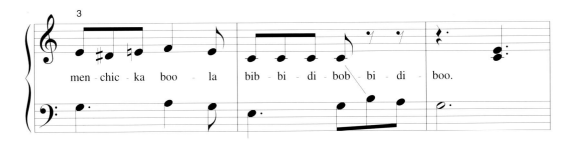

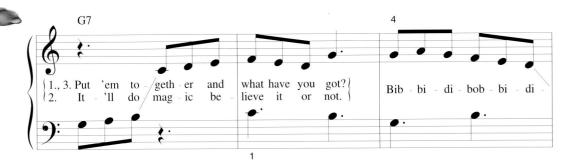

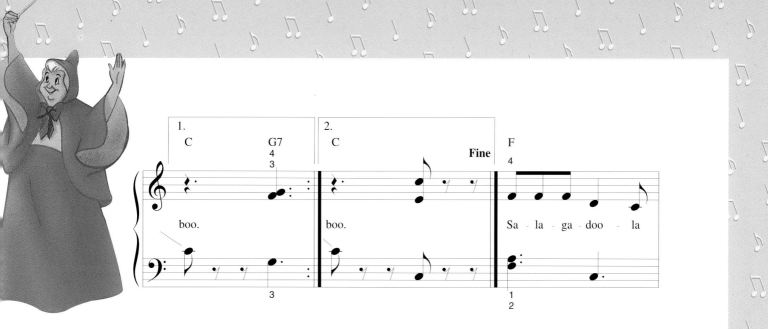

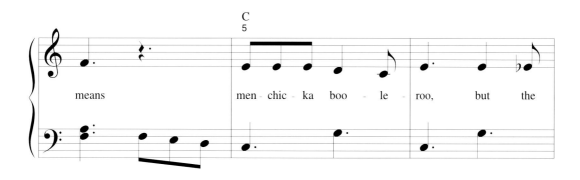

1.
C   G7
boo.

2.
C   Fine   F
boo.   Sa - la - ga - doo - la

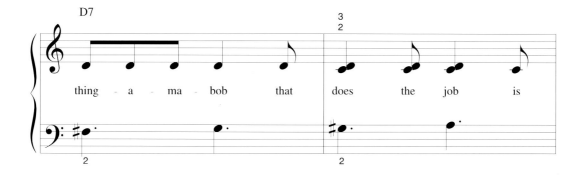

C
means   men - chic - ka - boo - le - roo,   but   the

D7
thing - a - ma - bob   that   does   the   job   is

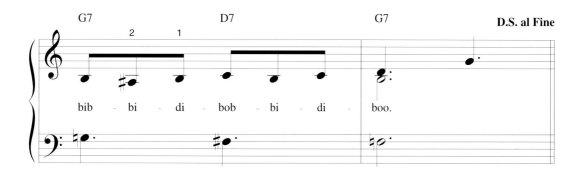

G7   D7   G7   D.S. al Fine
bib - bi - di - bob - bi - di -   boo.

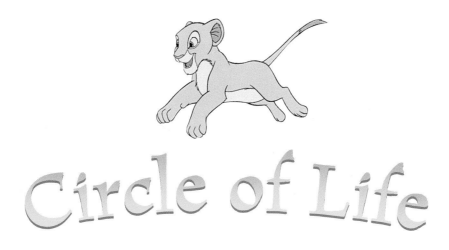

Circle of Life

From Walt Disney Pictures' *The Lion King*

Music by Elton John • Lyrics by Tim Rice

Moderately, with an African beat

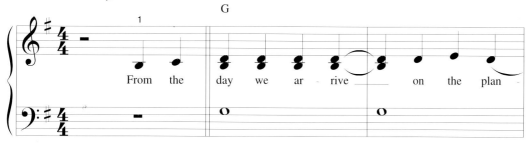

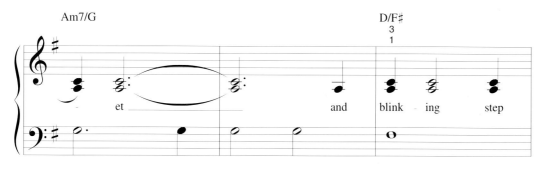

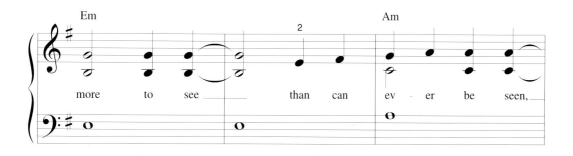

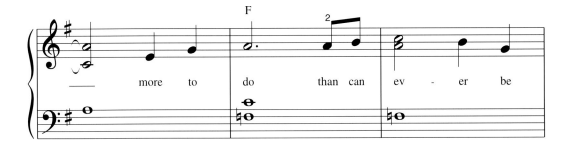

more to do than can ev - er be

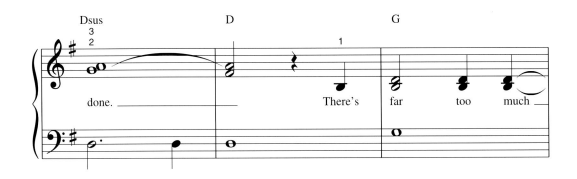

done. There's far too much

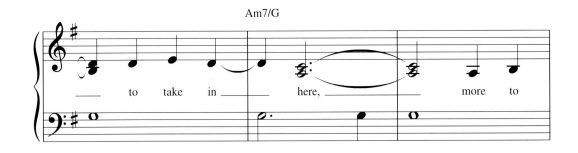

to take in here, more to

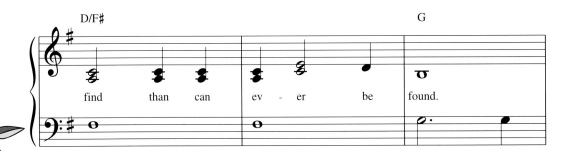

find than can ev - er be found.

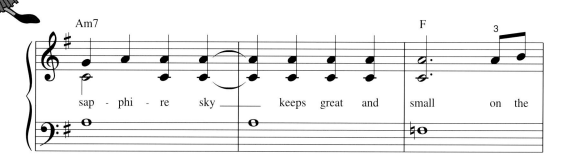

But the sun roll - ing high through the

cresc.

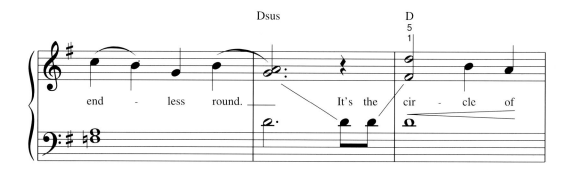

sap - phi - re sky _____ keeps great and small on the

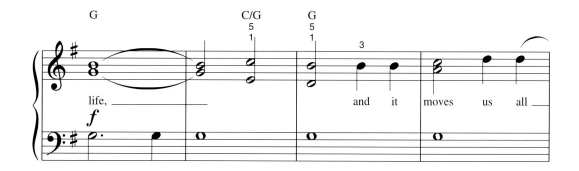

end - less round. _____ It's the cir - cle of

life, _____ and it moves us all _____

f

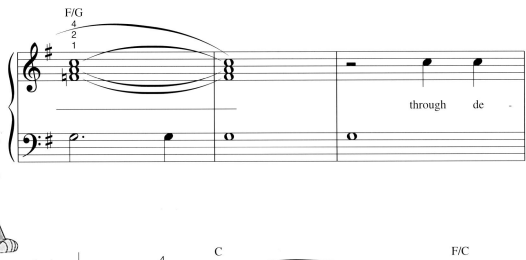

through de -

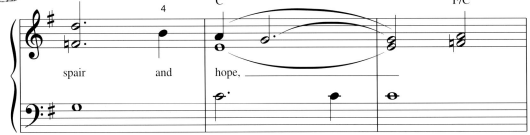

spair and hope,

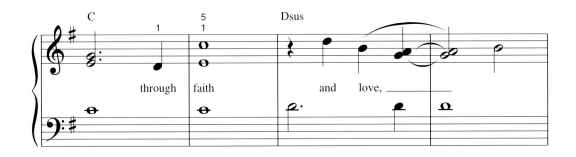

through faith and love,

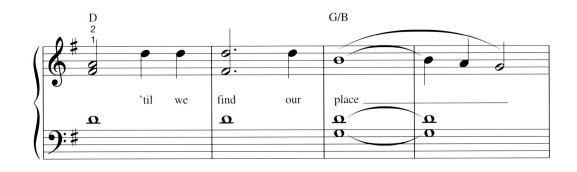

'til we find our place

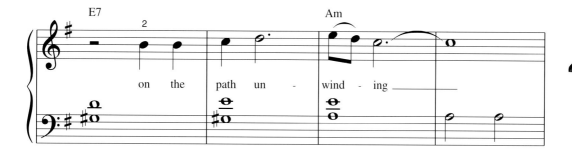

on the path un - wind - ing

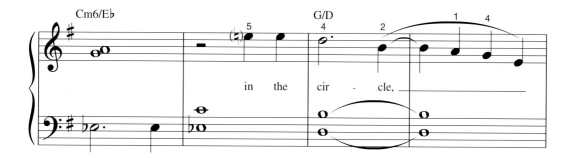

in the cir - cle,

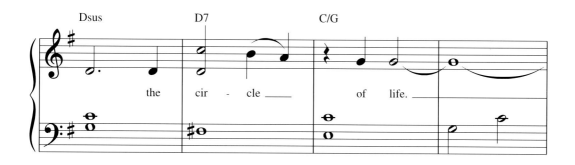

the cir - cle of life.

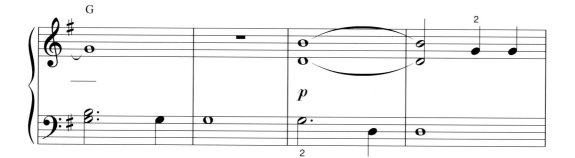

p

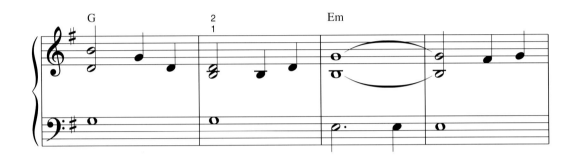

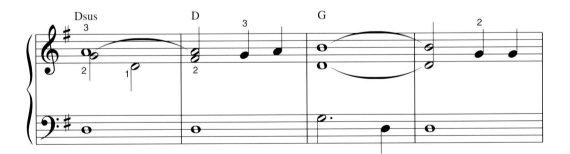

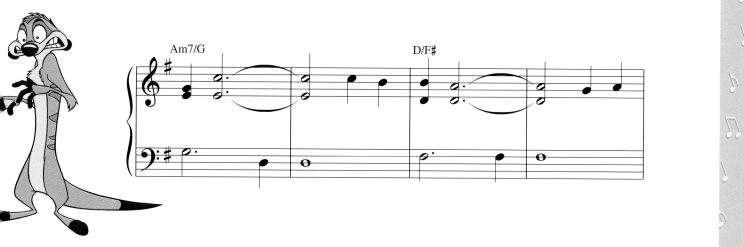

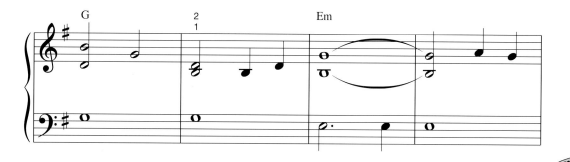

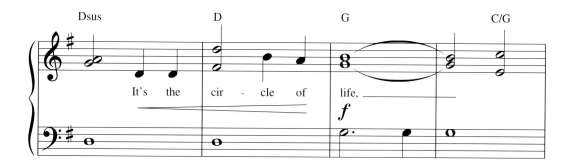

It's the cir - cle of life,

and it moves us all

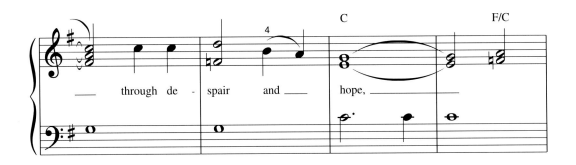

through de - spair and hope,

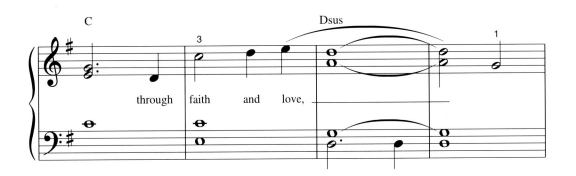

through faith and love,

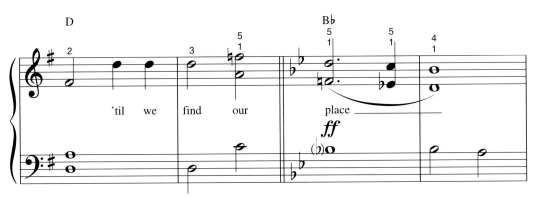

'til we find our place

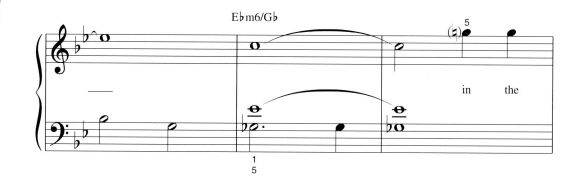

on the   path   un - wind - ing

in the

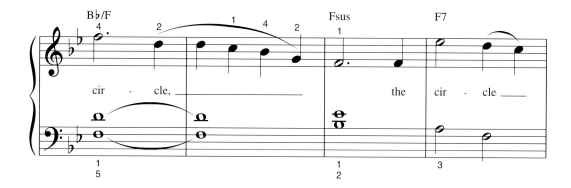

cir - cle, _____   the   cir - cle _____

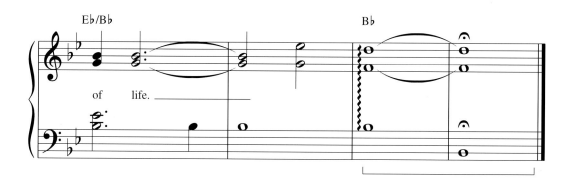

of   life. _____

Hakuna Matata

From Walt Disney Pictures' *The Lion King*

Music by Elton John • Lyrics by Tim Rice

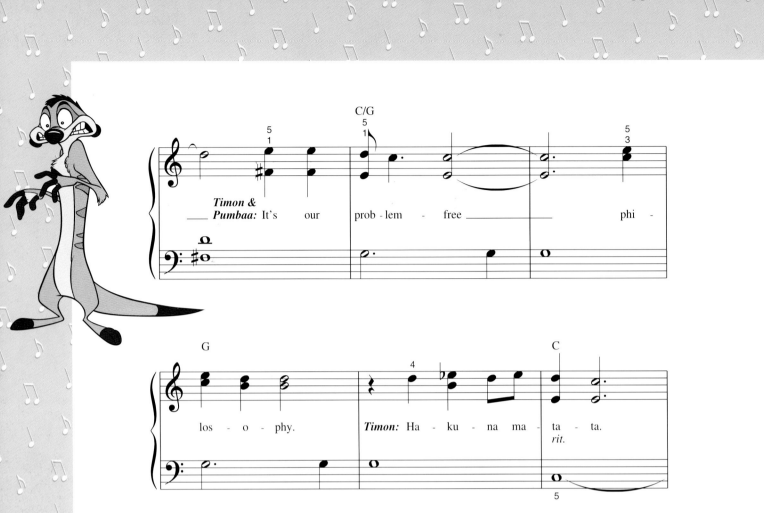

Timon & Pumbaa: It's our prob - lem - free _____ phi -

los - o - phy.   **Timon:** Ha - ku - na ma - ta - ta.
rit.

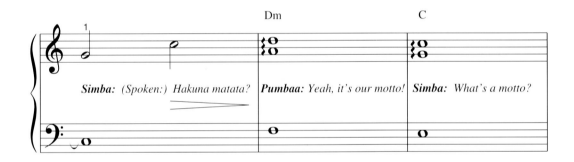

Simba: *(Spoken:) Hakuna matata?*   **Pumbaa:** *Yeah, it's our motto!*   **Simba:** *What's a motto?*

Timon: *Nothin'! What'sa motta with you? (Laughter)*   **Pumbaa:** *Y'know kid, these*

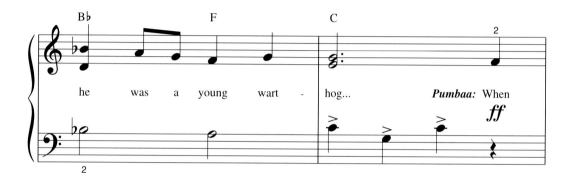

two words will solve all your problems. **Timon:** *That's right. Take Pumbaa for example. Why,* when

f

he   was   a   young   wart - hog...   **Pumbaa:** *When*

ff

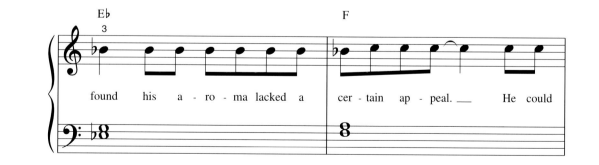

I   was   a   young   wart - hog!   **Timon:** *Very nice.*   **Pumbaa:** **Timon:**
rit.   *Thanks.*   He

mf

found   his   a - ro - ma   lacked   a   cer - tain   ap - peal. __   He could

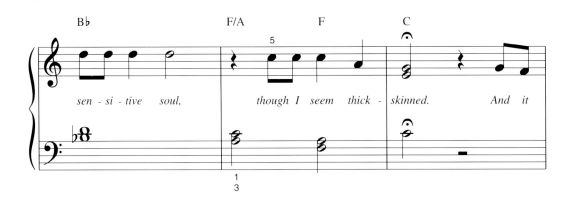

C   G

(Spoken:)
clear the sa - van - nah af - ter   *ev - 'ry meal!* **Pumbaa:** *I'm a*

Bb   F/A   F   C

sen - si - tive soul,   *though I seem thick - skinned.*   *And it*

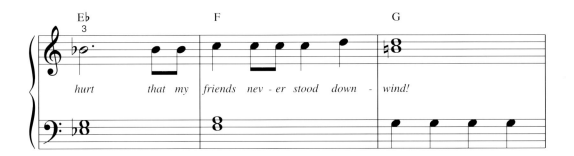

Eb   F   G

hurt   *that my friends nev - er stood down - wind!*

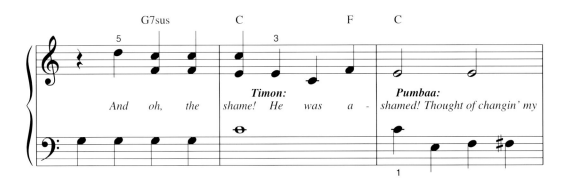

G7sus   C   F   C

And oh, the   *shame! He was a -*   *shamed! Thought of changin' my*

Timon: **Pumbaa:**

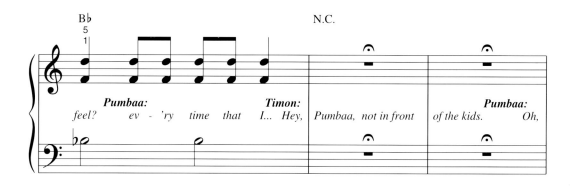

Timon:
name! Oh, what's in a

Pumbaa:
name? And I got down - heart - ed... How did you

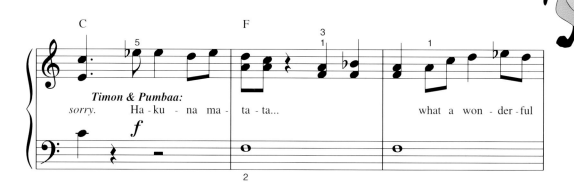

Pumbaa:
feel? ev - 'ry time that I... Hey,

Timon:
Pumbaa, not in front

of the kids.

Pumbaa:
Oh,

Timon & Pumbaa:
sorry. Ha - ku - na ma - ta - ta...

what a won - der - ful

phrase.

Ha - ku - na ma - ta - ta...

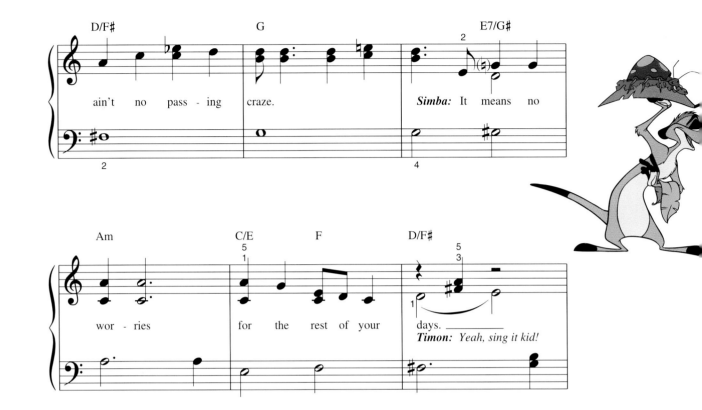

ain't   no   pass - ing   craze.

Simba: It   means   no

wor - ries   for   the   rest   of   your   days. _____

Timon: *Yeah, sing it kid!*

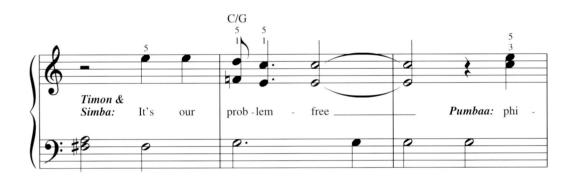

Timon &
Simba: It's   our   prob - lem   -   free _____   *Pumbaa:* phi -

los - o - phy.

Timon & Pumbaa:
Ha - ku - na   ma - ta - ta.

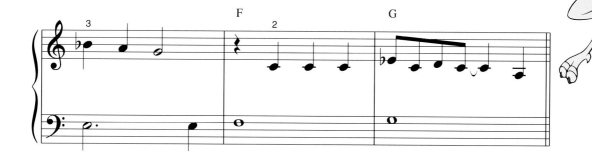

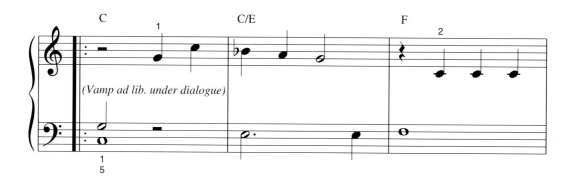

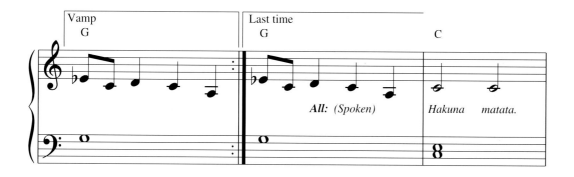

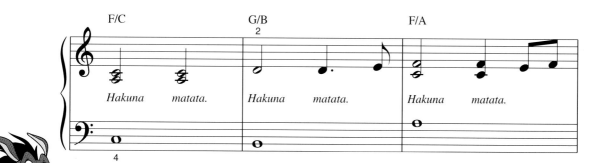

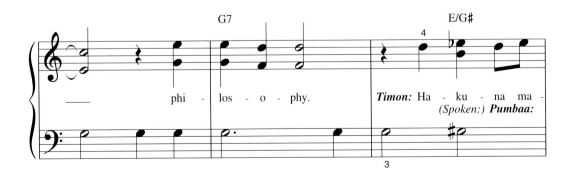

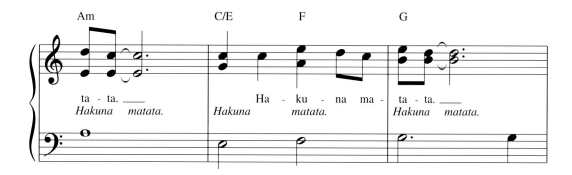

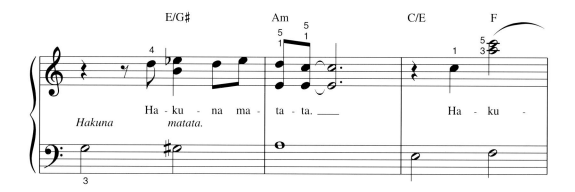

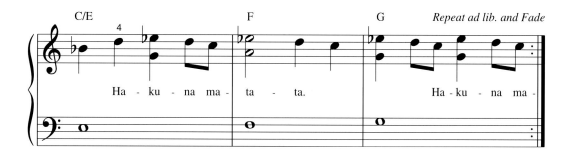

Beauty and the Beast

From Walt Disney's *Beauty and the Beast*

Lyrics by Howard Ashman • Music by Alan Menken

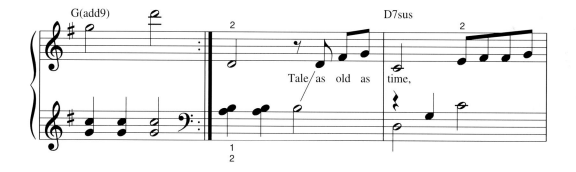

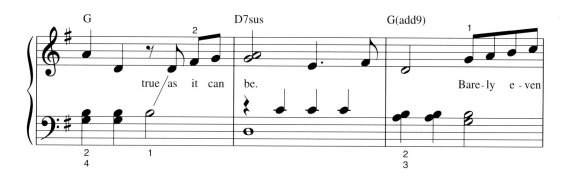

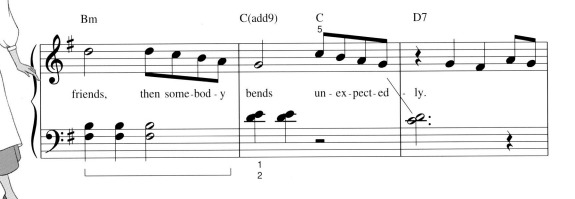

Bm   C(add9)   C   D7

friends,   then some-bod - y   bends   un - ex -pect-ed - ly.

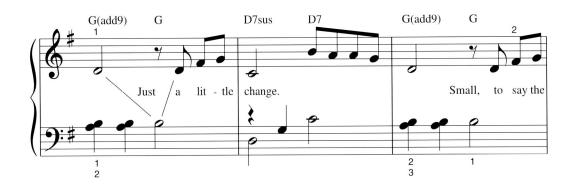

G(add9)   G   D7sus   D7   G(add9)   G

Just   a   lit - tle   change.   Small,   to   say the

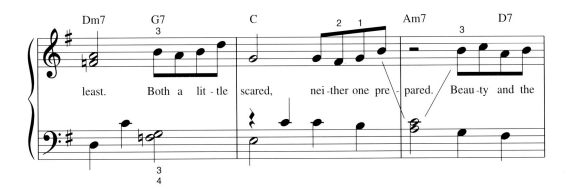

Dm7   G7   C   Am7   D7

least.   Both a   lit - tle   scared,   nei-ther one pre - pared.   Beau -ty   and   the

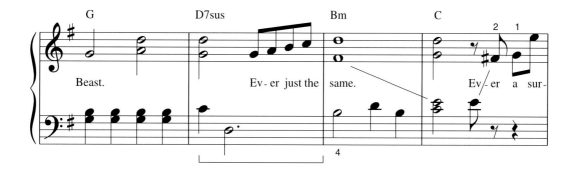

Beast.

Ev - er just the same.

Ev - er a sur-

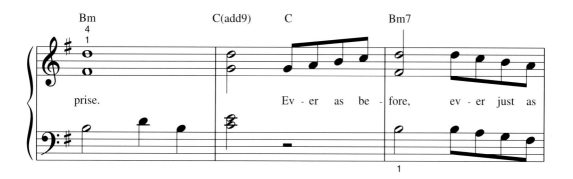

prise.

Ev - er as be - fore,

ev - er just as

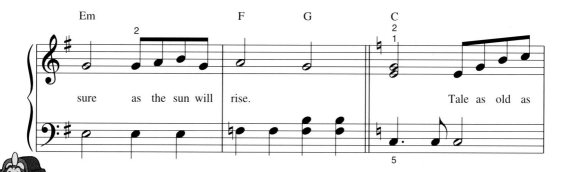

sure   as the sun will rise.

Tale as old as

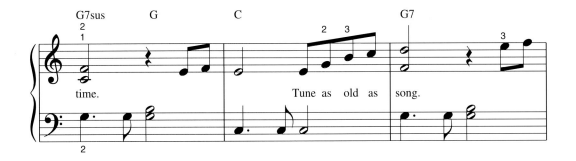

time. Tune as old as song.

Bit-ter-sweet and strange, find-ing you can change, learn-ing you were

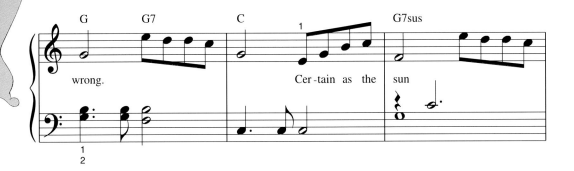

wrong. Cer-tain as the sun

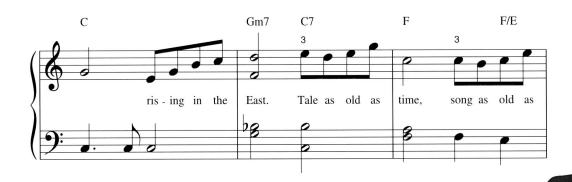

ris-ing in the East. Tale as old as time, song as old as

rhyme. Beau‑ty and the Beast. Tale as old as

time, song as old as rhyme. Beau‑ty and the Beast.

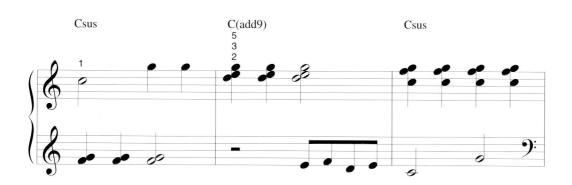

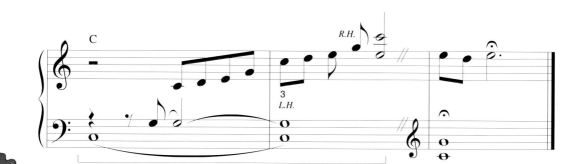

Winnie the Pooh

From Walt Disney's *The Many Adventures of Winnie the Pooh*

Words and Music by Richard M. Sherman and Robert B. Sherman

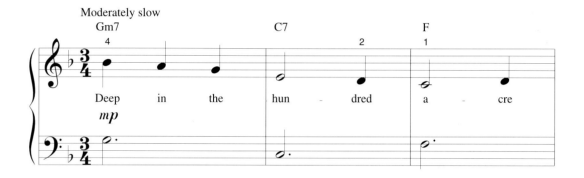

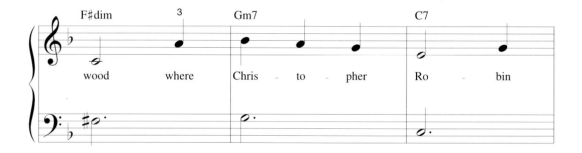

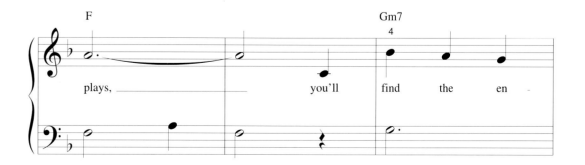

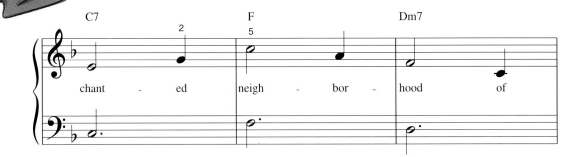

chant - ed | neigh - bor - hood | of

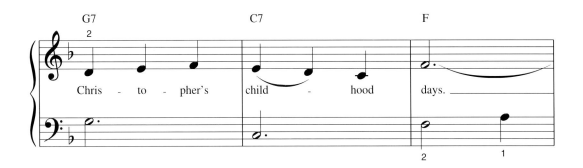

Chris - to - pher's | child - hood | days.

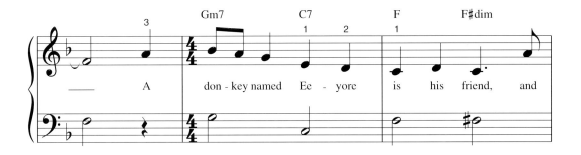

_____ A | don - key named Ee - yore | is his friend, and

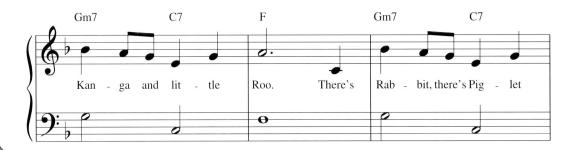

Kan - ga and lit - tle | Roo. There's | Rab - bit, there's Pig - let

and there's Owl, but most of all Win-nie the Pooh!

Win-nie the Pooh, Win-nie the Pooh, tub-by lit-tle cub-by all

stuffed with fluff, he's Win-nie the Pooh, Win-nie the Pooh,

wil - ly, nil - ly, sil - ly ole bear.

The Wonderful Thing About Tiggers

From Walt Disney's *The Many Adventures of Winnie the Pooh*

Words and Music by Richard M. Sherman and Robert B. Sherman

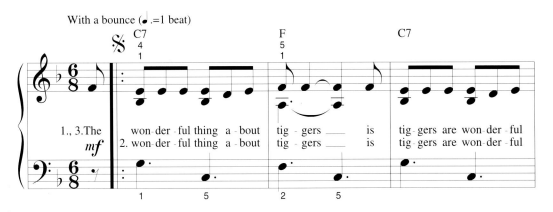

With a bounce (♪.=1 beat)

1., 3.The won-der-ful thing a-bout tig-gers ____ is tig-gers are won-der-ful
2. won-der-ful thing a-bout tig-gers ____ is tig-gers are won-der-ful

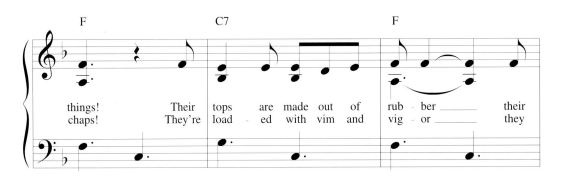

things! Their tops are made out of rub-ber ____ their
chaps! They're load-ed with vim and vig-or ____ they

bot-toms are made out of springs. ____ They're boun-cy, troun-cy,
love ____ to leap in your laps. ____ They're jump-y, bump-y,

foun - cy, poun - cy,
clump - y, thump - y,   fun! Fun! Fun! Fun!   Fun! _____   But the most won-der-ful   *p*

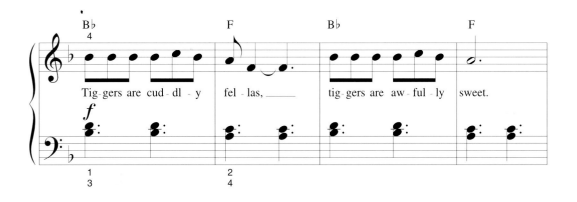

thing a-bout tig-gers is   *f*   I'm the on - ly   one!   Oh, the   one! _____   **Fine**

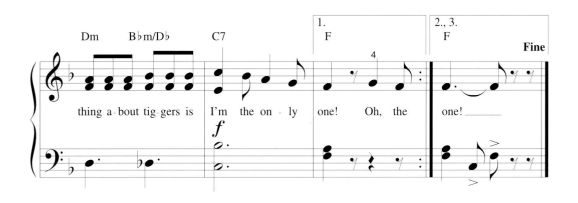

Tig-gers are cud - dl - y   *f*   fel - las, _____   tig-gers are aw-ful-ly   sweet.

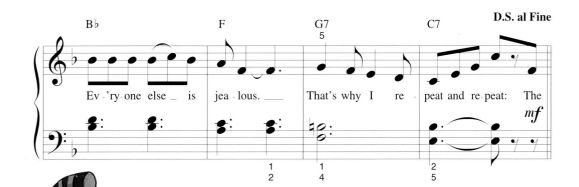

D.S. al Fine

Ev -'ry-one else _ is   jea - lous. _____   That's why I   re - peat and re-peat: The   *mf*

GO THE DISTANCE

From Walt Disney Pictures' *Hercules*

Music by Alan Menken • Lyrics by David Zippel

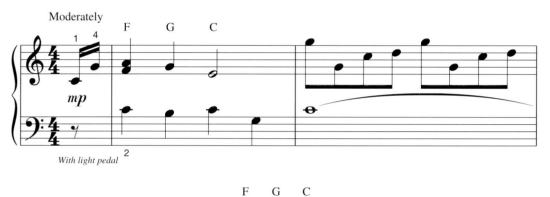

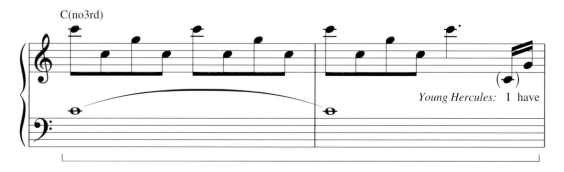

Young Hercules: I have

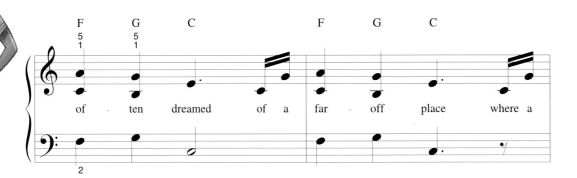

of - ten dreamed of a far - off place where a

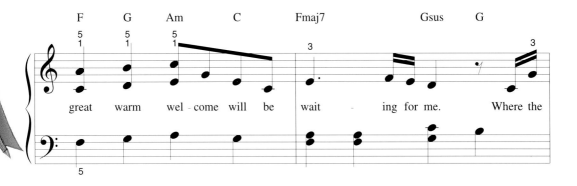

great warm wel - come will be wait - ing for me. Where the

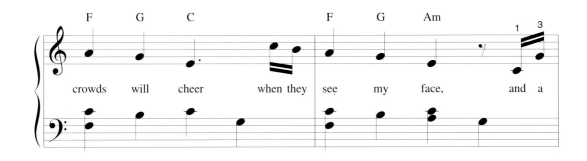

crowds will cheer when they see my face, and a

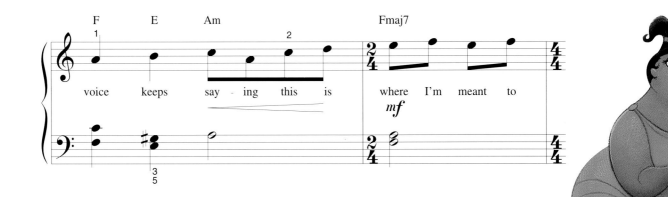

voice keeps say - ing this is where I'm meant to

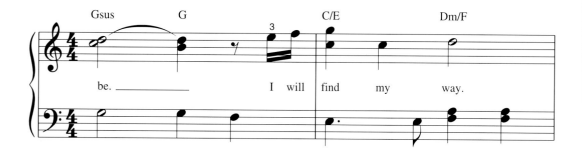

be. _____ I will find my way.

I can go the dis - tance. I'll be there some - day if I can be strong. I know ev - 'ry mile will be

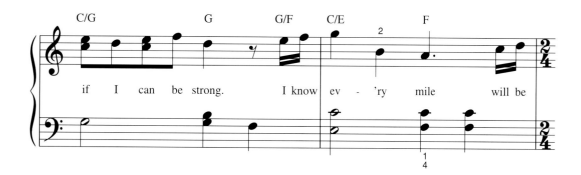

worth my _____ while. I would

go most an-y-where to feel like

I _____ be-long. I am

on my way. I can go the dis-tance. I don't

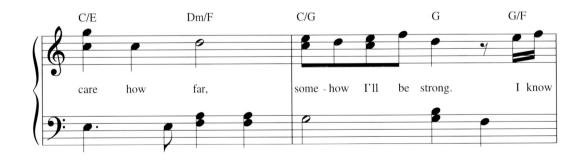

care how far, some-how I'll be strong. I know

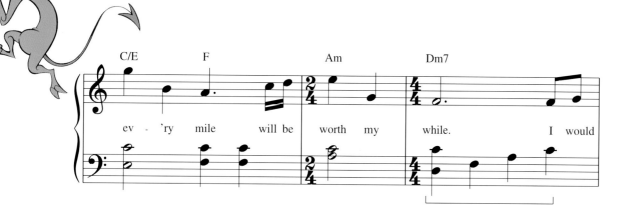

ev - 'ry mile will be worth my while. I would

go most an - y -where to find where I _____ be -

long.

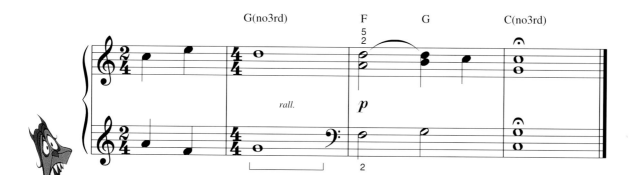

Printed in Hong Kong
First Edition
7 9 10 8 6
Library of Congress Catalog Card Number 97-66885
ISBN: 0-7868-3147-2 (trade) — 0-7868-5071-x (lib. bdg.)